# An Intervention

## by Mike Bartlett

The first performance of *An Intervention* took place on
16 April 2014 at Watford Palace Theatre

# An Intervention

## by Mike Bartlett

## Cast

| | |
|---|---|
| A | Rachael Stirling |
| B | John Hollingworth |

## Creative Team

| | |
|---|---|
| Direction | James Grieve |
| Design | Lucy Osborne |
| Lighting Design | David Holmes |
| Sound Design | Tom Gibbons |
| Assistant Direction | Kay Michael |
| Design Associate | James Turner |
| | |
| Production Manager | Matt Ledbury |
| Company Stage Manager | Maddie Baylis |
| Deputy Stage Manager | Alicia White |
| Assistant Stage Manager | Eleanor Butcher |
| Stage Management Placement | Anna Lambert |
| Costume Supervisor | Mark Jones |

## MIKE BARTLETT (Writer)

Mike is currently Associate Playwright at Paines Plough. In 2011 he was Writer-In-Residence at the National Theatre, and in 2007 he was Pearson Playwright in Residence at The Royal Court Theatre.

His play *Love, Love, Love* won Best New Play in the 2011 Theatre Awards UK, *Cock* won an Olivier Award in 2010 for Outstanding Achievement in an Affiliate Theatre, he won the Writers' Guild Tinniswood and Imison prizes for *Not Talking*, and the Old Vic New Voices Award for *Artefacts*.

His television series *The Town* was nominated for a BAFTA for Breakthrough Talent.

Theatre credits include: *Bull* (Sheffield Theatres/Off-Broadway); *Medea* – a new version (Headlong/Glasgow Citizens/Watford/Warwick); *Chariots of Fire* (Hampstead/Gielgud); *Love, Love, Love* (Paines Plough/Theatre Royal Plymouth/Royal Court); *13* (National Theatre); *Decade* (co-writer – Headlong); *Earthquakes in London* (Headlong/National Theatre); *Cock* (Royal Court/Off-Broadway); *Contractions* (Royal Court); *Artefacts* (nabokov/Bush/59E59 Theatre, New York); *My Child* (Royal Court)

Radio credits include: *The Core, Heart, Liam, The Steps, Love Contract, The Family Man* (BBC Radio 4); *Not Talking* (BBC Radio 3).

## RACHAEL STIRLING (A)

Rachael has been twice nominated for an Olivier Award for *An Ideal Husband* (West End) and *The Priory* (Royal Court).

Theatre credits include: *Variation on a Theme* (Finborough); *Medea* (Headlong); *The Recruiting Officer, Helpless* (Donmar Warehouse); *An Ideal Husband* (Vaudeville, West End); *A Midsummer Night's Dream* (Rose, Kingston); *The Priory* (Royal Court); *Pygmalion* (Theatre Royal Bath/Japan); *Uncle Vanya* (Wilton's Music Hall); *Look Back in Anger* (Theatre Royal Bath); *Tamburlaine* (Bristol Old Vic); *Theatre of Blood* (National Theatre); *Anna in the Tropics* (Hampstead); *A Woman of No Importance* (Theatre Royal Haymarket).

Film credits include: *Sixteen* (Seize Films); *Snow White and the Huntsman* (Universal); *Salmon Fishing in the Yemen* (BBC Film); *Centurion* (Pathe Pictures Int); *The Young Victoria* (Gk Films); *Dangerous Parking* (Comiche Pictures); *The Truth* (2 Many Executives); *Framed* (STV Films Ltd); *Triumph of Love* (Recorded Picture Co); *Another Life* (Another Life Ltd); *Maybe Baby* (Inconceivable Films); *Complicity* (Talisman); *Still Crazy* (Still Crazy Prod Ltd).

Television credits include: *The Game, Dr Who, The Haunting of Toby Jugg, Women in Love, Riot at the Rite, Tipping the Velvet* (BBC); *The Bletchley Circle, The Bletchley Circle 2, Boy Meets Girl, Lewis, Miss Marple – Murder at the Vicarage, The Quest III, Bait, Poirot – Five Little Pigs* (ITV); *Minder* (Talkback Thames); *Othello* (LWT).

Radio credits include: *Possession* (Pier Productions); *Hold Back the Night, The Pallisers* (BBC Radio 4).

## JOHN HOLLINGWORTH (B)

Trained at RADA.

Theatre credits include: *Our Country's Good* (Out of Joint); *Making Noise Quietly* (Donmar Warehouse); *Earthquakes in London* (National Theatre On Tour/Headlong); *The Deep Blue Sea* (West Yorkshire Playhouse); *Design For Living* (Old Vic); *The Power of Yes* (National Theatre); *Women, Power and Politics* (Tricycle); *Observe the Sons of Ulster Marching Towards the Somme* (Hampstead); *For King and Country* (Theatre Royal Plymouth/UK tour); *Playboy of the Western World* (Nuffield Southampton).

Film credits include: *Cinderella* (Disney); *About Time* (Working Title); *The Dark Knight Rises* (Warner Brothers); *The Burma Conspiracy* (Pan-Europeene); *Godard & Others* (Poppies Films); *Pelican Blood* (Ecosse Films); *Dorian Gray* (Ealing Studios).

Television credits include: *Our World War* (BBC 3); *Crossing Lines* (NBC); *Da Vinci's Demons* Season Two (Starz); *Breathless* (ITV Studios); *The Hour* (BBC America); *Endeavour, Wuthering Heights* (ITV); *London's Burning* (Channel 4) *The Man Who Crossed Hitler, Twenty Twelve, Casualty 1909, Being Human* (BBC).

Radio credits include: series of *Deadheading, Craven, Number Ten*. Other radio includes *Beryl – A Love Story on Two Wheels, Murder in Samarkand, The Tower* (BBC Radio Four) and *Adventures of the Soul* (BBC Radio Three).

John is filming a regular role in BBC One's upcoming *Poldark*.

**JAMES GRIEVE (Direction)**

James is Joint Artistic Director of Paines Plough. He was formerly co-founder and Artistic Director of nabokov, and Associate Director of the Bush Theatre.

His directing credits for Paines Plough include *Jumpers for Goalposts* by Tom Wells, *Hopelessly Devoted* and *Wasted* by Kate Tempest, *Love, Love, Love* by Mike Bartlett, *Fly Me to the Moon* by Marie Jones, *Tiny Volcanoes* by Laurence Wilson, *You Cannot Go Forward From Where You Are Right Now* by David Watson and *The Sound Of Heavy Rain* by Penelope Skinner.

Further credits include *Translations* (Sheffield Theatres/ETT/Rose); *66 Books: A Nobody* by Laura Dockrill, *The Whisky Taster* by James Graham, *St Petersburg* by Declan Feenan and *Psychogeography* by Lucy Kirkwood (Bush); *Artefacts* by Mike Bartlett (nabokov/Bush/national tour/Off-Broadway); *Kitchen, Bedtime for Bastards, Nikolina* by Van Badham (nabokov) and the world premieres of *Old Street* by Patrick Marber (nabokov Arts Club) and *The List* by David Eldridge (Arcola).

**LUCY OSBORNE (Design)**

Lucy's previous designs for Paines Plough include *Jumpers For Goalposts* (also Hull Truck, Watford Palace Theatre and Bush); The Roundabout Seasons (2011 and 2012) and *Love, Love, Love* (also Royal Court/national tour).

Her many other theatre designs include *Privacy, Coriolanus, Berenice* and *The Recruiting Officer* (Donmar Warehouse); *In the Vale of Health, Hello/Goodbye, Blue Heart Afternoon* (Hampstead); *Translations, Plenty, The Unthinkable, The Long and the Short and the Tall* (Sheffield Theatres); *The Machine* (Manchester International Festival/NYC); *Huis Clos* (Donmar Trafalgar Season); *Twelfth Night* (winner of the Chicago 'Jeff Award' for Scenic Design); *The Taming of the Shrew* (Chicago Shakespeare Theatre); *Peter Pan* (Sherman Cymru); *Precious Little Talent* (Trafalgar Studios) and *Shades* (Royal Court).

As an Associate Artist at the Bush Theatre her work included *The Aliens, Like A Fishbone, The Whisky Taster, If There Is I Havent Found It Yet, Wrecks, Tinderbox, Sea Wall*, The Broken Space Season.

**DAVID HOLMES (Lighting Design)**

David trained at the Theatre Royal Glasgow and the Guildhall School of Music and Drama.

Theatre credits include: *Backbeat* (Duke of York's, London/ Ahmanson, Los Angeles); *The Nutcracker* (Nuffield Southampton); *Fanny Och Alexander* (Malmo Stadsteater, Sweden); *Hello/Goodbye, Donny's Brain, Belongings* (Hampstead Studio); *King John, The Gods Weep, Days of Significance* (RSC); *Benefactors* (Sheffield Theatres); *A Midsummer Night's Dream* (Headlong/UK tour); A Philharmonia Orchestra WAGNER Charity Gala by personal invitation and in honour of His Royal Highness The Prince of Wales' 65th Birthday at Buckingham Palace; Wagner 200th Anniversary Concert, Berlioz *Romeo and Juliet* Concert, semi-staged production of *Bluebeard's Castle* (also European and US tour) and Gurrelieder and Dallapiccola's *Il Prigioniero* (for the London Philharmonia Orchestra at the Royal Festival Hall); *You're a Good Man Charlie Brown* (Tabard, London); *Moonlight and Magnolias, The Rise and Fall of Little Voice, Rope* (Watermill, Newbury): *Rememberance Day, Alaska* (Royal Court); Gogol's *The Government Inspector* (Young Vic/Taking Part); *Cat on a Hot Tin Roof* (Novello; London); *La Serva Padrona, To Hell and Back* (for Opera Faber at the Viana do Castelo festival; Portugal); *The Aliens, Cruising* (Bush); *Dick Whittington* (Lyric Hammersmith); *Victory: Choices In Reaction, The Road to Mecca* (Arcola); *The Chairs, Gagarin Way* (Bath); *How To Be Another Woman, Things of Dry Hours* (Gate); *Rusalka* (ETO); *Goalmouth* (Sage Gateshead); *Ma Vie en Rose* (Young Vic); *Cannibals, Widowers' Houses, A Taste of Honey, See How They Run, Pretend You Have Big Buildings, Cyrano De Bergerac; Harvey, Roots* (Manchester Royal Exchange); *Blood Wedding* (South Bank); *Sweetness, Badness* (WNO); *After Miss Julie, Othello, Woman in Mind, Be My Baby* (Salisbury); *Tilt* (Traverse, Edinburgh); *Hortensia and the Museum of Dreams* (RADA); *Humble Boy, The 101 Dalmations* (Northampton); *Stallerhof* (Southwark Playhouse); *Fijis* (for Jean Abreu Dance at the South Bank Centre and The Place); *Inside* (Jean Abreu Dance); *The Leningrad Siege* (Wilton's Music Hall); *The Trestle at Pope Lick Creek* (Manchester Royal Exchange/Southwark Playhouse); *The Fantasticks, Ain't*

Misbehaving, House and Garden, Cleo;
Camping; Emmanuelle and Dick
(Harrogate); The Secret Rapture
(Chichester); Twelfth Night (Cambridge);
Look Back in Anger (Exeter); Dov and Al,
The Water Engine, The Water Harvest,
Photos of Religion, A State of Innocence
(Theatre503).

## TOM GIBBONS (Sound Design)
Tom trained at Central School of Speech
and Drama.

Theatre includes: Happy Days (Young Vic);
Translations (Sheffield Crucible), Home
(Arcola); 1984 (Headlong/ Almeida);
Lionboy (Complicite); Grounded
(Gate/Traverse); As You Like It (RSC); Julius
Caesar (Donmar Warehouse); Hitchcock
Blonde (Hull Truck); The Spire (Salisbury
Playhouse); London (Paines Plough);
Roundabout Season (Shoreditch Town
Hall/Paines Plough); The Rover (Hampton
Court Palace); Love Love Love (Royal Court);
Island (National Theatre/tour); Romeo and
Juliet (Headlong); Disco Pigs (Young Vic);
Dead Heavy Fantastic (Liverpool
Everyman); Plenty (Crucible Studio,
Sheffield); Encourage the Others (Almeida);
Wasted (Paines Plough/ tour); Chalet Lines,
The Knowledge, Little Platoons, 50 Ways to
Leave Your Lover (Bush); Hairy Ape, Shivered,
Faith, Hope and Charity, The Hostage, Toad
(Southwark Playhouse); Sold (Theatre503);
The Chairs (Ustinov Bath); The Country, The
Road to Mecca, The Roman Bath, 1936, The
Shawl (Arcola); Utopia, Bagpuss, Everything
Must Go, Soho Streets (Soho); The Machine
Gunners (Polka); Fat (Ovalhouse/tour); Just
Me Bell (Graeae/tour); Fanta Orange, Blue
Heaven (Finborough); Rhinegold (The Yard).
As Associate: A Season in the Congo (Young
Vic); Choir Boy (Royal Court); Broken Space
Season (Bush); Shivered, Faith, Hope and
Charity, The Hostage, Toad (Southwark
Playhouse); Sold (Theatre503); The Chairs
(Ustinov Bath); The Country, The Road To
Mecca, The Roman Bath, 1936, The Shawl
(Arcola); Utopia, Bagpuss, Everything Must
Go, Soho Streets (Soho); The Machine
Gunners (Polka); Fat (Ovalhouse/tour); Just
Me Bell (Graeae/tour); Fanta Orange, Blue
Heaven (Finborough); Rhinegold (The Yard).

## KAY MICHAEL (Assistant Direction)
Kay is Paines Plough's director on
placement. She trained at Drama Centre
London and read English and Theatre
Studies at the University of Warwick (BA
First Class Hons). She is a founding
member of award-winning curious
directive with whom she has directed,
performed and devised.

Directing credits include: Clarion (Staged
Reading, PlayWROUGHT, Arcola); True Or
False (Theatre Uncut, Arcola); Smell
(Pleasance, Invertigo); Her Dying Wish
(Made from Scratch, Rich Mix); Freefall
(GSMD, Invertigo); The Lodger, Home
(Ovalhouse); Just One (Lost Theatre); The
Nth Degree (Off Cut Festival, Old Red Lion;
Rosemary Branch Theatre); Mercury Fur
(site-specific); An Ordinary Spectacle
(curious directive); Shoot Get Treasure
Repeat (Warwick Arts Centre).

Assisting credits include: Don Gil of the
Green Breeches (Theatre Royal Bath,
Arcola, Belgrade Theatre Coventry); Tender
Napalm (Southwark Playhouse); Return to
the Silence (Pleasance, curious directive); A
Midsummer Night's Dream (Milton Rooms);
Othello (Lauderdale House, Veni Vidi
Theatre).

Upcoming: UK premiere of Norwegian
playwright Arne Lygre's Then Silence, at
the Platform Studio Theatre.

## JAMES TURNER (Design Associate)
Credits as Designer include: The Hotel
Plays (The Langham Hotel); Our Ajax, I Am
A Camera, Execution of Justice (Southwark
Playhouse); Donkey Heart, Still Life/Red
Peppers (Old Red Lion); Cuddles
(Ovalhouse); The Long Life and Great Good
Fortune of John Clare (Eastern Angles
tour); John Ferguson, A Life, The Sluts of
Sutton Drive (Finborough); Strong Arm
(Underbelly, Edinburgh); Mercury Fur
(Trafalgar Studios 2 – 2013 Off-West-End
Award Best Set Designer); Thrill Me
(Charing Cross); Plain Jane (Manchester
Royal Exchange); A Man of No Importance
(Arts). Credits as Associate Designer
include: A View From the Bridge (Young
Vic); Jumpers for Goalposts (Paines Plough
tour). Credits as Assistant Designer
include: Mojo (Harold Pinter); Powder Her
Face (ENO); Gloriana (Royal Opera House);
The Recruiting Officer, Julius Caesar
(Donmar Warehouse); Children of the Sun,
A Comedy of Errors (National Theatre).

**'Revered touring company Paines Plough'** *Time Out*

Paines Plough is the UK's national theatre of new plays. We commission and produce the best playwrights and tour their plays far and wide. Whether you're in Liverpool or Lyme Regis, Scarborough or Southampton, a Paines Plough show is coming to a theatre near you soon.

**'The lifeblood of the UK's theatre ecosystem'** *Guardian*

Paines Plough was formed in 1974 over a pint of Paines bitter in The Plough pub. Since then we've produced more than 130 new productions by world renowned playwrights like Stephen Jeffreys, Abi Morgan, Sarah Kane, Mark Ravenhill, Dennis Kelly and Mike Bartlett. We've toured those plays to hundreds of places from Manchester to Moscow to Maidenhead.

**'That noble company Paines Plough, de facto national theatre of new writing'** *Telegraph*

We celebrate 40 years of Paines Plough in 2014 with our our biggest, boldest, furthest-reaching programme of work ever. Programme 2014 sees 10 productions touring to 50 places around the UK, featuring the work of 100 playwrights.

**'I think some theatre just saved my life'** @kate_clement on Twitter

Paines Plough Limited is a company limited by guarantee and a registered charity.
Registered Company no: 1165130
Registered Charity no: 267523

Paines Plough, 4th Floor, 43 Aldwych, London WC2B 4DN
+ 44 (0) 20 7240 4533
office@painesplough.com
www.painesplough.com

 Follow @PainesPlough on Twitter

 Like Paines Plough at facebook.com/PainesPloughHQ

Donate to Paines Plough at justgiving.com/PainesPlough

# **Paines Plough** are

**Watford Palace Theatre**

## Watford Palace Theatre...
is a local theatre with a national reputation.

The creative hub at the heart of Watford, the Palace engages people through commissioning, creating and presenting high-quality theatre, and developing audiences, artists and communities through exciting opportunities to participate. Contributing to the identity of Watford and Hertfordshire, the Palace enriches people's lives, increases pride in the town, and raises the profile of the area. The beautiful 600-seat Edwardian Palace Theatre is a Grade II listed building, busy with live performances and film screenings seven days a week, offering world-class art to the tens of thousands of people visiting the Theatre each year.

The quality of work on stage and beyond is central to the Theatre's ethos. Recently, the Palace has enjoyed critical acclaim for its productions of: Gary Owen's *Perfect Match* (2013) & *Mrs Reynolds and the Ruffian* (2010, TMA Best New Play nomination); Ronald Harwood's *Equally Divided* (2013); Neil Simon's *Lost in Yonkers* (2012) & *Brighton Beach Memoirs* (2010, TMA Best Supporting Performance in a Play nomination); and Charlotte Keatley's *Our Father* (2012).

Work created at Watford Palace Theatre regularly tours nationally. Recent co-productions include: *Jumpers for Goalposts* with Paines Plough and Hull Truck (Off West End Award for Best Male Performance and UK Theatre Award nomination for Best New Play); *Stuart: A Life Backwards* with HighTide and Sheffield Theatres; *Break the Floorboards* with Rifco Arts (Asian Media Awards – Best Live Event); *The Firework Maker's Daughter* with the Opera Group, Opera North and ROH2 (Olivier Award nominated); *Medea* with Headlong and Citizens Theatre, Glasgow; and *Stick Man* with Scamp, which continues to tour internationally.

The Palace has commissioned new plays from a range of exciting writers including: Charlotte Keatley, Tom Wells, Mike Bartlett, Danny Kanaber, Gary Owen, Stacey Gregg, E.V. Crowe and Tanika Gupta.

Projects such as *Black History Month* (2013), *Our Sound* (2013) and *Showtunes: Shuffled* (2013) have brought together the creativity of Watford's diverse communities. These build on the regular programme of Palace and Hertfordshire County Youth Theatres, adult workshops, backstage tours, community choir and extensive work with schools.

## With thanks to the Friends of Watford Palace Theatre

### Business Friends
Metro Printing, Warner Bros. Studios, Leavesden

### Good Friends
Anonymous, Frank and Helen Neale, Mark Parker, Norman and Mavis Tyrwhitt, Peter Freuchen

# Watford
## Palace Theatre
ON TOUR

Work created at and with Watford Palace Theatre regularly tours nationally. Productions you may have seen recently:

**Jumpers for Goalposts** a new play by Tom Wells, co-produced with Paines Plough and Hull Truck, recently playing at the Bush Theatre

**Stickman** from the book by Julia Donaldson, co-produced with Scamp, which toured internationally and played at London's Soho and Sound Theatres and the Edinburgh Festival

**Stuart: A Life Backwards** co-produced with HighTide Festival Theatre and Sheffield Theatres, which toured nationally and played at the Edinburgh Festival

**Break the Floorboards** co-produced wth Rifco Arts, which toured nationally

**The Firework Maker's Daughter** co-produced with the Opera Group, Opera North and ROH2, which toured nationally and played at London's Royal Opera House

**Medea** co-produced with Headlong and Citizens Theatre, Glasgow, which toured nationally

**Ballroom of Joys and Sorrows**, co-produced with Kate Flatt Projects and Greenwich Dance in association with English Folk Dance and Song Society, which toured to Greenwich, London

**Tiddler and Other Terrific Tales**, co-produced with Scamp Theatre, which toured nationally

**Bunny** by Jack Thorne, a Fringe First-winning production in association with nabokov and the Mercury Colchester, which toured nationally and played at London's Soho Theatre and in New York

**Britain's Got Bhangra** conceived and written by Pravesh Kumar, music by Sumeet Chopra, lyrics by Dougal Irvine, co-produced with Rifco Arts and Warwick Arts Centre

**Family Business** a new play by Julian Mitchell, co-produced with Oxford Playhouse

 twitter.com/watfordpalace

 facebook.com/watfordpalace

**www.watfordpalacetheatre.co.uk**

# AN INTERVENTION

Mike Bartlett

*For Tiberius Ren*

4

**Characters**

**A**
**B**


*The play takes place in front of curtains – like Morecambe and Wise, or Abbott and Costello. Only the bare minimum is brought on for each scene.*

A *and* B *are designations for speech, not names.*

*The two characters must be quick and clever but can be played by actors of any age, gender or ethnicity.*

*The genders of the pronouns in the play should be changed accordingly.*


*( / ) means the next speech begins at that point.*

*( – ) means the next line interrupts.*

*(…) at the end of a speech means it trails off. On its own it indicates a pressure, expectation or desire to speak.*


*This text went to press before the end of rehearsals and so may differ slightly from the play as performed.*

# 1.

## Harmonica

A      Oh.

B      Yeah.

A      You –

B      Yup.

A      Wow.

B      Yes.

A      I don't believe it.

B      Well it's true.

A      You would would

B      Support it.

A      Support it

B      Yeah.

A      You *would*?

B      Yeah.

A      Wow.

B      (*nods*)

A      I don't believe it.

B      Okay.

A      Jesus.

B      Shall we stop now?

A      Jesus *Christ*.

B      Yes.

A      Fuck *off*.

B      Right

A      Shit a *brick*. You're telling me you would?

B      Not sure how else to put it.

A      I didn't –
       I never –
       You would.

B      I would.

A      You would *support an intervention*.

B      Yes.

       *Pause.*

       A *turns to the audience.*

A      I always look forward to seeing him, he's got a kind of
       relaxed air, keen to talk about one of the new books
       he's bought, not academic or obsessive not overly
       detailed, he's read the kind of books you get on the
       bookshop table at the front, the kind of popular
       science, sociology, military historical books the easy
       ones that accompany a documentary on the Discovery
       Channel, with a title that's a question: '*Was Kennedy
       Gay?*' '*What's the Point of Men?*' that kind of thing.
       And it's amusing, having him in my life as this low-
       rent provocateur, but it's precisely this trait, which up
       till now I liked, this relaxed populist oppositional
       thinking, saying the vaguely controversial thing for the
       sake of it, that is now the problem. Because it's that
       table of non-thoughts, those glib opportunistic books,
       which have caused this idea to congeal in his head,
       which have given him evidence upon which he's now
       basing this completely misguided very wrong opinion.

B      Actually, not just 'would support it'.

A      What?

B      I do support it. I actively want it.

A      Oh no.

B      Because you know if all those people we're talking
       about over there if they all had white skin, like in Poland
       in the Holocaust, or Bosnia in the nineties, you'd be all

for getting in there and sorting it out. That's the real reason why you think it's not your problem, because those people over there, all of them, are brown.

A     Brown.

B     Subconsciously, you think it's a different culture. More primitive. So – their fault. *Ergo* – their problem. Why have you got a harmonica? Did you take it to the thing?

A     You want a drink? I want a big drink. I want a drink that has a very big high kind of outrageously large percentage alcohol content. *Because they're brown?!* I want to drown my sorrows, no I want to drown you, I want to damage your interior organs. You should be punished for your despicable views. You should have a pint of something deadly like absinthe or meth.

B     I'd prefer port.

A     You... port? You want *port*?

B     If you're offering.

A     Now?

B     Yeah. It's late.

A     It's *nine o'clock*.

B     Exactly.

A     you should get out more.

B     I know.

      *Beat.*

A     Since when did you drink port? What are you? *French?* All these revelations I thought we were best friends.

B     (*laughs*)

A     What?

B     Ha!

A     What?

B     Funny. Best friends...

A     ?

B        Oh. Wait I thought you were... you know like really
         only small children have best... But you're...

A        ?

B        No okay best friends fine. Yup. Have you done
         something with the carpet in here? Lovely pattern.

A        You don't think we are?

B        We've only known each other three years

A        What's that got to do with it?

B        Don't get me wrong we have a good time, we get on
         but I mean, well...

A        What?

B        I have lots of friends.

         *Beat.*

A        I don't have a port glass.

B        A wine glass is fine.

A        A wine glass of port? That's what you want?

B        No a normal amount of –

A        I thought *I* had the drinking problem.

B        I don't mean you should *fill the glass*, just –

A        Except, of course, actually, I don't. *I don't* have a
         drinking problem. That's just what you tell me.

B        Come on, I didn't mean a drinking problem drinking
         problem, just that sometimes you like a drink and
         that's fine but when you do, there's another and
         another and things get, you know. Dropped. Like
         ornaments. And manners.

A        Okay, so you want a wine glass of *port*, which will
         hopefully give you liver disease, and I'll *obviously*
         have a pint of tequila because I have that *drinking
         problem* – the advantage of which will be that I'll then
         be incapable of calling an ambulance when you choke
         on your vomit, because from where I'm standing either
         of those two endings, slow liver failure or sleepy vomit

is about what you deserve, since our country is about to slaughter thousands of people in the Middle East and since *you* couldn't be bothered to do a fucking thing about it, well woop-de-shit let's both have the biggest amount of booze we've ever had, *YES,* this could be *fun.* Back in a minute.

A *leaves.* B *turns to the audience.*

B    She's an inspirational human being.

Not because she's a brain surgeon or a human rights lawyer, I mean she's just a teacher just a normal teacher teaching... actually I don't know what she teaches... it's kids. She teaches kids, but really she could have been anything because the fact is, what's completely captivating about her is that from the moment she walks in a room, she's clever and on you and won't let you off the hook. And from the moment we met I think we realised that we did things for each other; she energised me and fired me up, and I soothed her steadied her I think and gave her perspective. And yes since then we've been really close really good, important friends –

A *returns.* B *paces.*

A    Here. An ocean of port. Now calm down.

B    Can't believe you're drinking tequila.

A    I'm not going to drink a *pint of tequila* don't be obscene. It's wine.

B    What wine?

A    Pinot. Sauvignon. Something. What are you doing?

B    You don't know which wine?

A    I'm not middle class like you.

B    I'm not expecting you to be middle class I'm expecting you to read the label.

A    Why won't you stand still?

B    Don't know what you mean.

A    Parading around.

| | |
|---|---|
| B | Thinking. |
| A | Be still. |
| B | Is it a problem for you? If I choose to walk like this? |
| A | Just so long as you're relaxed. |
| B | All right. |

*Beat.*

| | |
|---|---|
| A | Go on then. |
| B | *What?* |
| A | Relax. |
| B | I am. |
| A | doing that thing with your hand. |
| B | What thing? |
| A | Your shoulders are all |
| B | Well they are *now* of course they are *now* get off me! Leave me alone and I'll... *Leavemealone!* |

*Beat.*

| | |
|---|---|
| A | Alright. |

Now.

Tell me exactly why you want to invade this country and kill everyone?

| | |
|---|---|
| B | Not me. |
| A | No? |
| B | No, *I'm* not killing anyone, if you *listened*, I'm saying I *support* – |
| A | Yeah but you don't have to march in there with a semi-automatic and kill the kids yourself – |
| B | Are you okay? |
| A | Yes I'm fine – you don't have to lay the illegal cluster mines with your own hands, if you're giving them support then – |

B     You look a bit sad

A     Well I'm *passionate* –

B     Are those tears?

A     *This matters.*

B     No, we've talked about controversial things before, and you've never – I mean you're quite *contained* normally.

A     *Contained?* No. Contained is like the opposite of me. I don't know what you mean. Contained. Ridiculous.

B     I mean you generally don't give away how you're feeling.

A     What? I give *everything* away.

B     Well

A     I'm *Mediterranean*!

B     You – Are you?

A     Originally. You really think I'm not passionate?

B     No I didn't say not passionate

A     It's one of my *main things*.

B     Yes of course, your hands waving, when you get worked up, the funny facial expressions

A     Right. Exactly. Wait. Facial expressions? What facial expressions?

B     Right – like that – I mean I'd assumed that it's a performance, the rolling eyes, the cheeks, because it's what you do with abstract ideas. Opinions. The tears on the other hand, like those we saw just now, only happen when it's closer to home – When it's family. Friends.

A     You're saying I'm selfish now? Things only matter to me if I'm personally involved

B     That's normal. If I was in a car crash you'd feel it more keenly than if it was someone else in a car crash who you never heard of.

A     Hmmm I don't know, I think I'd feel a lot more sorrow
      for a perfectly decent stranger I hadn't previously met
      than the good friend, if not best friend, I unfortunately
      *have previously met*, who's standing in front of me
      calling me an alcoholic and advocating a *big war.*

B     The moment you found out your mother had died,
      when your sister had the miscarriage

A     Why are you bringing that up?

B     those are the only two moments I've seen you cry
      like this

A     I'm *not crying.*

B     Despite what you think, I do know you.

A     Clearly not.

B     You want a hug.

A     Stay away from me. Get off.

B     Come on. Now you're sulking, that's the next stage.

A     I'm *not* don't treat me like a child you're just trying to
      *distract* me from the fact you've become Hitler.

B     Okay.

A     Pol fucking *Pot.*

B     Okay.

A     Is this an experiment?

B     Hmm?

A     A kind of devil's-advocate thing like you do with your
      students – trying to bring out the argument in me by
      taking a completely *ludicrous* right-wing position?

B     Don't need to bring the argument out in you, look at
      you go, must be because you're *Mediterranean*

A     You really mean this neo-con shit?

B     no not neo-con but yes I do believe we have a moral
      obligation to go in and stop the killing yes, whatever
      the colour of their skin.

A    With guns.

B    If it's the only way, which I think this time, it is

then yes.

*Beat.*

A    Is that a moustache?

B    What?

A    Just… a trace of hair just…

B    I haven't got a clue what you're talking about.

A    (*to the audience*)

We were meeting in Leicester Square so we could all walk down together – and it was a stupid place to meet as I'm saying it I know that we should have chosen somewhere much less crowded, but anyway eventually we got it together and the five of us were there, and I was like where is he? And they said, he never got back to us, and I was like, no no, if anyone is coming, if I would put money on *anyone* coming to attend a march against something like this, it would be him, because, I said, he gets it, he's truly compassionate, and you know what? I got them to wait – I was so sure he would turn up, I got them all to stand there for twenty minutes until they eventually they were like 'he's really not coming' and I looked like a prick.

B    What do you mean?

A    I mean when I was standing there waiting for you –

B    What do you mean a *moustache*?

A    I mean there's a moustache under your nose, a little pencil-thin dictator-like, warmongering –

B    Oh okay, I get it.

*Beat.*

I didn't say I was coming. Never said that.

A    I thought I knew you well enough to assume –

B    If you'd bothered to ask –

A     Facebook?

B     If you'd actually bothered to call.

A     You should have seen it today.

B     I saw it on TV

A     You should have *been there*.

B     With the Marxists and the anti-Semites and the islamo-fascists, and the dictator apologists, no thanks, fine as I am.

A     Sat there on your couch

B     I wasn't *sat there* –

A     You mean you watched it *standing up*? Weird.

      I'll bet you didn't even manage that. Got bored, thought no one'll know, flipped it over, on with the porn –

B     It's me.

A     What?

B     I'm *me* here, the me you know the same me. There's things we've not agreed on before.

A     Yeah but this is different.

      B *looks closely at* A.

B     I don't think it's just this that's the problem.

A     What, it's not enough? Our country goes to war because you can't be bothered to get up off your apathetic arsehole and stop it, because you'd rather sit there and crank one out

B     I wasn't 'cranking / one out'

A     rather do *whatever* you were doing than lift a finger to make a difference and you're saying that that's not enough to justify my irritation?

B     No your bottom lip tells me that the problem is much closer to home than the Middle East.

A     My bottom lip *is* the Middle East.

| | |
|---|---|
| B | Okay – *what*? |
| A | That's what all of this, my face, how I'm feeling, the Middle East is entirely what it's about, nothing else. |
| B | I don't think that's true. |
| A | … |
| B | |
| A | I brought the harmonica to play. |
| | I thought since it was a protest it might be appropriate that in some way it could maybe add to proceedings but before you ask no there was never a moment, it turned out it wasn't really that kind of thing. |
| B | |
| A | What? |
| B | How drunk are you? |
| A | How does that matter? |
| B | I'm trying to gauge whether to bring something up or whether to leave it till the morning. |
| A | Four. |
| B | Four? |
| A | Yeah. |
| B | You seem a bit further down the… |
| A | Down the? |
| B | I mean up, up the scale, higher than four is what I'm – |
| A | I had one earlier and this, I've eaten dinner, I've been out all day, I've been on adrenalin not booze I'm a four. Four. Four. |
| B | Okay, if that's really what you think you are then – |
| A | Test me. Give me a word. If you don't believe me. Give me a really difficult word to say. |
| B | No we don't have to do that. |
| A | Come on, it'll be good. |

B        Honorificabilitudinitatibus

         *Beat.*

A        Is that Latin?

B        Shakespeare. Honorificabilitudinitatibus. It means –

A        Doesn't matter what it means.

         A *thinks*.

         Say it again.

B        Honorificabilitudinitatibus

A        Honorifica – bilitudini – bus.

B        That's actually

A        Right. Not bad. So. Four. *Four*. Means you can tell me.

B        Is it Hannah?

A        I – What?

B        Why you're crying.

A        *Hannah?*

B        Yeah. What you're really talking about tonight. Why you're – like that.

         *Beat.*

A        *Hannah?*

B        Okay so maybe it's not.

A        *Hannah?*

B        Forget it.

A        I've been out *all day*

B        not all day

A        because I *care* because this *matters to me*, that we are about to commit to sending our troops into harm's way, *again*, and not just that, but use our bullets and bombs that *we paid for*, to kill men and woman and children in another country who have not attacked us, and I'm out there out there *all day* fighting this –

B    Not all day –

A    All *afternoon* fighting this, and I magnanimously then
     invite you over to my house to my flat, to defend your
     absence, at which point you have the gall, the huge
     shiny testicular *balls*, to state that all that I'm feeling,
     it's not to do with military intervention really. No. It's
     about *Hannah*.

B    It's just you don't like her very much.

A    I don't… care about her right now.

B    You've seemed a bit jealous recently.

A    I'm not getting into this. *Jealous?* Of what? No.

B    Alright maybe not jealous but you've

A    What are you talking about?

B    Since her and I have got a bit closer I think things have
     got more difficult between the two of us.

A    THEY HAVE NOW! This was nothing to do with that.
     You can do what you like. *Hannah?* You would never
     even ask me anything like that before today, you know
     I'd never stop you doing anything, I'd never tell you
     who to be with – you're trying to deflect away from
     the issue – *Hannah* isn't important, you said it
     probably won't last.

B    Are you sure?

A    *Yes*. What? Am I sure what?

B    That you're a four, because it was exactly this reaction
     that I was hoping to avoid –

A    Oh no *I'm not a four*, I lied. Do I *look* like a four? I
     can barely *stand*. I'm an *eight* at least. After the march
     we went to a bar and I drank a lot, but you wouldn't
     know that because you *weren't there* but yes I am
     smashed, off my trolley, off my face, I am leathered,
     tight, hammered and sunk. I'm a LUSH, I'm probably
     a nine more than an eight but if you were the person I
     thought you were you would know that because you
     would have been there today, and even if you weren't

there today you'd see it in me tonight, and even if you
didn't see it in me tonight, that I'm this drunk because
I *care*, then we should have been able to *talk* about it,
but instead you think that all this is going on because
for *some reason* you've recently decided to start
sleeping with and touching and generally hanging
around with *Hannah* who, by the way, makes no
attempt to hide her contempt for your friends, who
*flirts with your mother*, and who looks like an *ant*.

B      An ant?

A      An ant yes, and yes I was a bit surprised when you two
were doing things, but not nearly as surprised as today
when you didn't turn up to protest with me. *This* is the
problem, *what you think about this government-
sanctioned act of colonial fucking terror –*

A *suddenly moves and pushes* B *away. It's sudden and
shocks them both.*

B      Hey!

A      Sorry.

B      You... hit me –

A      I... pushed, you I know I –

B      you *hit* me.

A      Pushed. It was a push. It was like –

B      GET OFF

A      I'm *demonstrating* – Okay I'll mime it. A push is like...

A *pushes in mid-air –*

That's a push, and a hit is like –

B      What are you doing?

A      Trying to show you the difference.

B      Are you going to say sorry?

A      I... I think I already did.

Okay.

'Sorry.'

Okay?

*Beat. They look at each other.*

Maybe you should go

Before this gets any more horrorificabilitudin –

– bus.

B    Yeah.

A    …

B    Yeah.

Okay.

I mean. It's late, so –

A    Just past nine not really.

B

A    Sorry.

B    See you then.

A    Yeah.

B    …

*He goes.*

A    Shit.

A *sips the port.*

Shit.

A *looks at the harmonica.*

*Feels a bit stupid.*

*Turns to us.*

There was once this man called Casper, he was called that because when he was born, he was very pale, and had this big round head and his parents thought 'oh! He looks like Casper the ghost' so that's what they called him, they thought it was cute, but unfortunately

after he'd been called that he continued to suffer from
anaemia and continued to be very pale, and his hair,
although it grew a bit was light and wispy and never
really covered his head in the right way, so at school
and as he grew, the name Casper became a taunt that
the other children shouted at him, they also called him
things like Mr Big White Baby, and Sir Tit Head and
these insults got to him and when he was thirteen he
discovered alcohol and enjoyed that a lot, so much so
that he drunk it all the time and there wasn't much his
parents could do to stop him, and it made him happy
and they thought it important that he make his own
mistakes so they didn't say anything. He grew up a
few more years till he was about seventeen, he liked
the drink so much that he even played the harmonica
less which if I'd been telling this story properly I
would have seeded at the beginning, that all he really
wanted was to be a harmonica player and the ironic
problem was that he couldn't drink and play the
harmonica at the same time, and they were his two
favourite things, and he'd lock the door of his room in
the evening, so his parents couldn't get in and he didn't
want to go out, because people would shout at him in
the street that he was a fat pasty balloon boy so he
stayed in, and if you were outside listening you might
hear this sound…

A *picks up the harmonica. She plays it, interspersed
with drinking.*

But he couldn't do both at the same time. So
eventually there was less of this.

*Harmonica.*

And more of this.

*Drink.*

Just a tiny bit of…

*Harmonica.*

But lots of…

*Drink.*

And eventually he drank so much that he didn't see any reason not to open his veins and let out the small amount of blood he had left, and he lay there in his room and died.

And in the morning he was found by his mother in bed, but he was so pale anyway that it took her ages to realise that as well as being unconscious he was also dead.

I was at school with him.

Casper. We didn't. We didn't know what had happened.

Until assembly one day.

Shit.

I want some crisps.

Sorry, that was a bad story and told even worse because I'm incredibly embarrassingly drunk.

But the important thing is the moral and the moral of it is that life is really difficult, and I understand why people drink.

A *downs the drink*.

**2.**

**Art**

*A and* B *enter and both look at the picture for a moment.*

*Pause.*

A      It's good.

B      Hmm.

A      Isn't it? Don't you think? Quite striking.

B      Right.

A      Not the usual sort of thing you have in a place like this, it's much more… Politicised.

B      …

A      For art I mean… it's quite…

       You want me to apologise. Is that it?

B      For what?

A      Ever since we met today there's been this cloud this doom hanging around my head like I killed your dog or something

B      I don't have a dog.

A      Like I murdered your aunt

B      What?

A      I could really do without this whole Berlin Chinese security wall of silence that's gone up since last time.

B      No. There's no…

A      You're not offering anything. In this conversation, I'm doing all the running it's like playing tennis I hit the balls over and you just watch them, you don't lift the racket you just watch them go past and offer monosyllabic comments 'oh' 'no' 'yes', it's like playing tennis with a fucking postbox.

B      Postbox.

A      Like trying to play tennis with that monolith from
*2001*, just sat there doing absolutely nothing, right there
in the middle of the court, the monolith, tennis racket
stuck on the side. And I'm like the Wimbledon theme
running about 'da da d'da, da da d'da', hitting all the
balls, you're like *Thus Spake Zarathustra* 'daaaa, daaa,
daaa' – yeah? Standing completely still as these balls
fly around. You know what I mean? No? No?

B      (*to the audience*)

Since that night, and I think this is why it's taken so
long for us to see each other, but whenever there's
been a text message from her, or the phone goes and I
see it's her calling, I hesitate and that's long enough for
me not to answer the phone. I don't know if she's
noticed, but the fact is that since that night, something
changed and now, this is terrible but whenever I have
to have contact with her, there's a bit, not a lot, but
there's a little bit of dread.

A      What did I do? That evening.

B      You don't remember?

A      I remember being angry because you didn't come on
the march, because you said you *approved* of what's
going on.

B      That's right.

A      I don't know whether that's still what you think but –

B      Yes it is.

A      Well… Okay, doesn't matter, you're entitled to your
opinion it's no excuse for bad behaviour, so I want to
say, formally, here and now, I'm sorry if I offended you.

B      You didn't offend me you were just very drunk, you
said some things I don't think you meant, I left, and
then presumably you ate some crisps put on the TV
and fell asleep.

A      No actually.

B      No?

A          I didn't have any crisps.

B

A          I'm sorry that I pushed you as well.

B          It was just a shock, I've never seen you hit anyone
           before

A          push.

B          Either way, there's no need for the apology.

A          You don't want it?

B          I just don't think there's a need for it.

A          What's going on?

*A moment.*

*They look at the picture.*

It's not real. That's not really Blair standing in front of
an exploding building taking a picture of himself on a
phone. It's been constructed as a comment on the Iraq
war and his culpability in taking us in there.

B          You thought I'd like it?

A          I thought you might learn from it.

B          *learn* from it? In that case there must be more to it than
           the glib Photoshop joke that meets the eye. If there's
           something to *learn* I assume there's an intricate and
           well-researched essay written in tiny letters
           somewhere, hidden away

A          Huh. No. –

B          Or is it one of those magic-eye pictures, if I squint, will
           it suddenly melge itself into something subtle and
           morally complex like the issue it's talking about. Wait –

A          Look…

B          I'm trying but this doesn't feel good.

A          Don't then.

B       Is it a magic-eye picture?

A       No.

B       You sure?

A       STOP IT. It's a nudge, I hoped this image might
        remind you of Blair, and Iraq

B       I didn't support the invasion of Iraq.

A       The *principle* of it.

B       Right, so you think that from now on, since you
        brought me here, the image will stick in my memory
        for ever and will slowly change my view of this
        intervention, even though it's a completely different
        country, a completely different situation and has
        absolutely nothing to do with Tony fucking Blair.

A       Why are you being like this?

B       There is no *principle*, there can't be because this is the
        world, not some essay by a twelve-year-old Oxbridge
        wanker on the *Guardian* blog.

A       How's Hannah?

        *Beat.*

B       Good.

A       And?

B       …

A       Come on.

        *Pause.*

        You said there was something to say.

        *Pause.*

B       She doesn't want me to see you.

A       She…

B       She thinks you're out of control. She said when you're
        dealing with an alcoholic

A     You think I'm an –

B     She thinks you are, but that you don't realise it yet.

A     Well thanks for this advice, I'll –

B     No, hold on, *she* thinks this, not me, I'm *quoting her*, okay, let's make that clear

      Is that clear?

A     Whatever.

B     No. Not whatever. This is important. Not me. Her.

A     Okay.

B     Sure?

A     Just tell your story.

B     So *she* said that when you're dealing with an alcoholic, which she thinks you are, from knowing you a bit over the last few years, seeing you at parties or whatever, she says that when you're dealing with an alcoholic the most important thing is that you don't indulge their behaviour, you don't stand over them and laugh, when they fall over, instead you just simply say 'you fell over', you don't normalise it, you make sure you reflect their behaviour back to them

A     You're a patronising arsehole.

      That's not rude I'm just reflecting your behaviour back to you.

      Carry on

B     She knows this about alcoholics because her dad is an alcoholic so she feels very strongly about the situation.

A     Does she agree with the war?

B     What's that got to do with it?

A     Does she advocate our military activites with the same enthusiasm as you? Yes or no.

B     She thinks it's right to go in and stop it yes.

A    It's called reinforcement. People seek out people with similar opinions to make themselves feel comfortable.

B    Don't be ridiculous it's nothing to do with that.

A    Well she doesn't want you to see me any more. Isolate these alcoholics from their friends, is that part of the system?

B    Of course not.

A    I'm not an *alcoholic*, I don't *use it*, I like it. Exactly the same as you.

B    Well, yes, I mean actually I think you're right, sometimes you drink more than is perhaps ideal, and that means you lose control I particularly thought that after you *hit* me

A    Define hit.

B    But with her – well, I think it's always been more of a personality clash between the two of you.

A    That I've got a personality and she looks like an ant?

B    What is this? The ant thing?

A    The ant thing's not the issue, how she looks isn't my problem, my problem is that she's the sort of person who stands at the side of the party, and doesn't do anything *interesting* or fun, but instead she'll take a picture of those that do, which if we're honest nine times out of ten is – me – or someone like me – she'll take a picture of us she'll put it on Facebook or tweet it and comment some passive-aggressive shit like 'someone was having a good time', and it's not a flattering picture ever, it's a picture of someone like me who works hard and doesn't get to enjoy myself that often, having a good time, and I could do without her little... comments. Honestly, go to her page have a look, she's like the fucking joy police, the fun Stasi, going round taking pictures –

And you know what? I refuse to curtail my behaviour, like everyone does now, because those are the

moments that life is all about, when you're
embarrassing, and wrong, and maybe sometimes a bit
illegal and ever since there's all these cameras you get
the feeling we've all stopped living a bit, and Hannah
is a fucking stormtrooper in that regard.

You never even liked her anyway.

B     We got on.

A     You got off. Historically, that was all it was, but after
that night when we argued, ever since then you've
been with her all the time.

B     Well I'm happier. I'm happier now. Aren't I? Don't I
seem happier?

A     Different yes. More relaxed maybe. 'Happier' yeah.
And anyway look, I don't mind what you do, she's the
one dishing out rules about who you're allowed to see.

B     Exactly, I know, and she's wrong, and I'm not going to
not see you, but I can't just ignore it. Can I?

It's going to be really difficult if you and her always
have to be separate.

A     Talk to her about it then.

B     I'd rather talk to you.

A     Why?

B     I just wonder if for the next few months, as things go
on, if we all see each other, if you could, just... tone it
down a bit.

A     Have less fun?

B     Just not drink so much, don't make her feel stupid.

A     She is.

B     At least respect her.

A     Hmm – Last time we met she tried to persuade me that
medical surgery was often completely unnecessary,
that sometimes it's not the internal organs that go
wrong, it's their *energy* and if we used, applied, the
right *stones*, sorry – *pebbles* – on the skin, instead –

B      Yes alright, it's easy to –

A      And I said do you think that'll work with the soliders out there being maimed and ripped to pieces and she said I know you're being glib but actually it might? They should give it a go. She said that, she actually thinks they should *give the fucking pebbles a chance*.

B      Try.

       I know she's not the same as you but –

A      Certainly she isn't.

B      Just don't –

A      Can one be empty and thick at the same time?

B      You said it yourself since I met her I've been a lot happier, we've been together two months, her and I, and already it's had this transformative effect. It really has. Whereas I've been friends with you for three years and

A      What?

B      Oh. Doesn't matter. All I'm saying is there's obviously something about her that makes me happier.

A      You're saying I don't make you happy?

B      No that's not – alright yes, I don't think that that's particularly what we do for each other: happiness.

A      We have fun.

B      Fun, but not... contentment. You and me, we're more about – truth.

A      So you like Hannah because she's not truthful, you like her because she sort of perpetuates a lie

B      Well, maybe you don't need to call it a lie, but on some level, yes possibly there's a comfort in her simplicity.

A      I'm sure she'd love to hear you saying this – simplicity...

B      I'm not expressing this well. You said yourself I was happier. So something's gone right. Hasn't it?

A Because you're not facing the truth any more.

B Yes. *Yes.* Okay. Maybe I want some comfort, for a bit. But that's okay. You *know* I haven't been *happy* in the past, for fuck's sake you helped me out through that, and now I am a bit better, and you're – for the sake of not having a drink you won't make a fucking effort I don't understand it.

A *Okay.* I will.

*Pause.*

B You will.

A Yes. If you want me to.

*Beat.*

Because it's you.

And you asked.

I'll 'tone myself down'.

*Pause.*

B Thanks.

*Pause.*

A You ever wonder if you were the tipping point? Because there must be a number that would have made a difference that day and a number that wouldn't. Enough people there, protesting, it would have had to stop it. And do you ever think that maybe that person could have been you, and you could actually have swayed it, if you'd come along. I know it sounds stupid, but sometimes –

B Please. Not now.

A Not now okay but these young men and women you're sending they have relationships too. They have husbands and wives and kids.

B They're soldiers that's what they signed up for, that's how it works I do my job they do theirs, and morally and for the world I actually believe we should try to stop the killing, and the maiming, and the rape, and the videos of people *eating each other.* That's what I think yes, and at the same time my best friend and my girlfriend seem to have a mutual hatred. Those two things are happening and I refuse to not feel one of them because of the other. Life carries on over there, and over here, at the same time. So? There. I've talked about it now. Let's move on.

**3.**

**Canapé**

*A enters with a table. On the table is a tray of canapés, and two wine glasses.*

A       It was a weird day that we met. The middle of the summer and yet it was raining, really hard, and the effect of this was that everyone who had arranged to meet friends for summer drinks ended up inside, and so the inside of the pub was very full.

And something about the weirdness of the weather meant that unusually we all started talking to each other. This never happens, but I suppose it was like we'd been through something, together. Anyway, I was with a group, and he was with a couple of other friends, and the two groups mixed, and we got talking, me and him, and – I'd had a couple and I told him that there didn't used to be a colour blue. That if you look back in the Greek myths, in the *Odyssey* and the *Iliad*, there isn't a specific word for 'blue' that separates it from 'green', and I said this is interesting because it's also one of the last colours that babies recognise.

I was saying this just out of interest, just making conversation, but he immediately replied 'no that makes no sense you're saying we don't see a certain colour until a certain stage of maturity, well alright, but so what, you can't compare biological maturity with maturity of a species? It's nonsense'. And it was delivered like that in such a patronising way that we started to argue, and while everyone around us was talking about the weather or football, we were really going for it about the *colour blue*. We had a great time.

And realised that in the arguing we were actually quite similar. We've argued ever since. And loved it.

I'm friends with a few of his colleagues. We've met at various pub meetings, or on Facebook, and last week I messaged them. I said you do know he supports the war? And they messaged back some of them and were like, no way. Really? Him? Of all people…

I hoped they might put some pressure on him. About this.

Not a lot of pressure.

But a bit.

B *enters*.

You interested in this?

B   No I don't mind, you can switch it off.

A   I thought you'd want to see, seeing as you were in *favour*. Thought we could sit down, all three of us, watch it together, with dinner, what do you think?

B   Is that why you chose tonight, to invite us over?

A   What?

B   Timed it with the invasion.

A   Er. They only decided to launch the missiles a few hours ago, whereas I invited you guys round last week, I wanted to give you plenty of notice, so unless you think I've got special access with the Ministry of Defence –

B   I hope not.

A   – or hacked my way into the Pentagon or something? But that would be quite a risk to take simply to correctly time a dinner party for ironic effect.

B   I bought you some port, you know to make up for –

A   Where is she?

Outside? Parking the car, you don't have a car. Is she scared? I don't bite.

B   She's not coming.

A   You promised.

B   In the end she thought it wasn't going to work.

*Beat*.

A   But I've *toned down*. I haven't touched a drop, I've learned not to swear, I've worn clothes that are a bit less… you know, a *bit less*. I've even cooked food that wasn't too spicy in case it was just *extremes* in general that she had a problem with. I made a very mild curry and I hate mild curry I think having a mild curry is a contradiction in terms, more than that, a *complete waste of* time.

B     She's also not feeling very well.

A     Er – you're supposed to give the excuse *before* the real reason?

B     Yes alright. She just doesn't want to spend an evening with you, is the truth.

*Beat.*

A *switches off the television.*

A     And what does she think about you coming over to see me on your own, with all my bad influence?

B     She's actually thought about it and reckons it's good that I stay in contact with you. She's worried that otherwise you might start shutting down socially.

A     Really.

B     That in your condition you might do something stupid.

*Beat.*

A     You know what. Let's abort. Here's the abort button. Big, red and shiny and I'm pressing it. It's pressed. Done. Go home.

B     No come on, I'm here, this is a chance for us to spend some time together.

A     Yeah, right, yeah mate, maybe we can touch base or catch up.

B     Exactly.

A     There was a dollop of sarcasm lurking in there think you missed it.

B     I ignored it.

A     Why?

B     Because I'm tired of irony, and sniping and snarking and I want –

A    No come on that's the fun. That's what clever people do because sincerity is boring.

B    No I think the opposite, that all of that *irony, all the time*, is juvenile. It doesn't do anything. It's just privilege to mock everything, to not really invest in anything positively. It's pure luxury to constantly pull down and never build. That's why satire dies in times of economic crisis.

     *A laughs.*

A    Did you just hear that last sentence?

B    It's true.

A    I'm sure.

B    I did a paper on it.

A    Love you sometimes…

     *Beat.*

     Don't go.

     *Beat.*

     Canapés?

B    What are they?

A    Mini fish and chips.

B    You made them?

A    Yes.

B    Wow.

A    No. Sorry that's a lie. I didn't. Make them. They're from Iceland. The shop. Not the. Very cheap. *Very* cheap. Frozen. Originally. But not now. They're nice. So. What do you think?

B    I'm fine thank you.

A    Don't be a snob.

B    I'm watching my weight.

     *A eats one.*

A    Hmm.

What do you see in her?

Hannah.

B     A huge amount.

A     What?

B     Lots of things. Too many to say –

A     So there's a list?

B     No.

A     A figurative list.

B     Well. Yes. There could be. If you want.

A     Go on then.

B     You want me to tell you?

A     Yeah just run down it for me.

B     I suppose in the end, what it really is –

A     No. No. The list.

B     Don't be stupid, I'm telling you, what it boils down to

A     Don't boil.

B     I think I love her –

A     *No!* You *said there was a list I want it all.*

B     Her *legs* then, her face, her eyes, her sense of humour, her wit

A     Humour and wit are basically the same thing

B     Her figure, her hair –

A     Okay so five of these have been physical.

B     Are you going to keep interrupting?

A     Yes.

*A eats another canapé. Gestures to carry on.*

B     Her intelligence, her demeanour but most of all the thing I like the most is the two of us, her and me what we do for each other, how we get on.

A        Do you see your friends these days?

B        What? Yes.

A        Go out for drinks with your colleagues as often as you used to?

B        Absolutely. Why?

A        No reason. You sure you don't want any of these? They're really nice.

B        Positive.

*A eats another canapé. Making a point, but getting quite full now.*

*Swallows.*

A        Hmm-mm. You know she sent me an email? Hannah.

B        What's your point?

A        Defensive. The email was nice, but it was brief. It said that she was sorry for me, and that she cared for me and wanted me to know that help was there if I needed it, and then – and this is the really funny bit. She put a link to *AA*, not the automobile association, in case you think she's worried about me breaking down –

B        Jesus

A        Well she *is* worried about me breaking down but just not in my car, no, there was this link, and it wasn't like some personal link, something that she could offer, it was just the front page of the Alcoholics Anonymous website which was a bit, like, if it meant so much to her to send this email, couldn't she even be bothered to find some specific person or number and not just link to the front page like I'd never even *heard* of Alcoholics Anonymous, like that would be a new concept to me.

B        At least she cared.

A        Well maybe. Thanks for the bottle of port by the way, since she's not coming shall we crack it open? I put the wine glasses out already just in case. Yeah but anyway my theory is she only sent this email so that she could tell you, so she could demonstrate some kind of faux

|   | compassion for me, she did tell you right? This isn't the first time you've heard about this email is it? |
|---|---|
| B | Look, can we just have a good night? I don't want to spend the whole time having a go at her, that won't be fun for me |
| A | There you are. |
| B | Thanks. |
| A | So none of your colleagues have said anything out of the ordinary. |
| B | Why are you asking me that? |
| A | Conversation. You see them as much as you used to? |
| B | Yes. |
| A | You don't see me as much as you used to. |
| B | Alright well obviously now I'm in a relationship, there's different priorities. |
| A | Ah, so you don't see your friends so much? |
|   | B *sighs, frustrated.* |
| B | Generally, these days, I see the people I want to see just the right amount. |
| A | You... Okay. Interesting. Good. Because I suppose these days you have a good time with her instead? |
| B | The best. |
| A |   |
| B |   |
| A | Oh! Come on! You're right! Why are we talking about *her*, why should you and me spend our entire time talking about someone that isn't here, especially on the night that your *team* go into action, you should be watching the TV. Apparently they say this is going to be unlike any war before, that technology has meant we will not even recognise this as conventional warfare, which sounds a bit creepy to me. |

B        They mean the targets, computers are better, they're
         less likely to hit the wrong thing, a lower amount of
         collateral damage, surely you're in favour of that.

A        Yeah but they're still basically going to be trying to
         take over the country.

B        What's for dinner?

A        Nothing if you don't have one of these.

B        I don't want one of those.

A        Only one left.

B        I'm fine. You *go for it.*

         A *looks at it. Really doesn't want it.*

A        No come on I've eaten them all myself, that's silly.

         You should have one.

B        Really.

A        It's only polite if nothing else.

B        It's from Iceland.

A        Exactly. Hmm. Come on.

         A *holds it up.*

         It's tiny.

B        No.

A        Eat it.

B        You going to force me?

A        What's the problem? Just eat it.

         A *puts it close to* B*'s mouth.*

B        No. Look. Really, get off me.

A        In it goes.

         B *suddenly slaps* A*'s hand away and the canapé falls
         on the floor.*

         Hey! What are you doing?

B        you were trying to force it in my fucking mouth!

A        I was playing, we used to do that stuff all the time.

         A *picks up the canapé from the floor.*

         *Dusts it down.*

         I won't see it go to waste.

B        Put it in the bin.

A        Ten-second rule.

B        You have it then.

A        Well I will if I have to but are you sure you don't want it?

B        You're joking.

A        Alright then.

         A *braces herself.*

         *Beat.*

B        Go on.

A        Give me a minute.

         A *second, then* A *eats the last canapé.*

B        Good?

         A *nods. Winces.*

         Are you…

         A *nods again, swallows, in pain, then –*

         *Makes a strange noise.*

         *Then –*

A        Leave her.

B        What?

A        Hannah.

         You're not suited. You and her. No one thinks so. You were lonely and she was keen and that's really the only reason you two are together. I'm sorry but I'm your friend and it has to be said.

B        What do you mean no one? 'No one thinks so'

A        Just that I messaged some of your friends to tell them
         about your view on the war, I thought it was only fair
         that they know, and we got talking, and the subject of
         Hannah came up, and they were very honest and the
         fact is, they hate her too, they think she's terrible and
         I'm only telling you this because I love you.

B        You've been talking on... what?

A        Facebook. Yeah. Look I know I'm not supposed to get
         involved like this cos if you don't leave her now it'll put
         me in a really difficult situation but it's got to the point,
         she's lied enough about me, she's done things, she's
         acted in a rude way, and I don't want to be one of those
         friends who only says it after, I'm declaring it now for
         better or worse that's the strength of our friendship: You
         are going out with a harridan a fucking bride of satan
         she is a nightmare, I've actually had dreams about her
         and I'm not even with her, and you know what my
         biggest fear is, is that you'll propose or she will and that
         will be it and the two of you will be together and you
         really need to know this – she is a class-A horrible
         woman, person, she is. She only wants you for the
         wrong things. We all think this, all of us, nearly
         everyone you know, including your mother, and okay
         now I've said it I know this might be the end of our
         friendship but someone had to say to your face what's
         being said behind your back, and now I have I'm
         counting on a sort of loyalty, on the fact that you know
         me and know I wouldn't say all this unless I loved you
         and wanted the best for you and really meant it.

         *Beat.*

B        When the phone goes and I see it's you, I don't answer
         any more. You know why?

A        She told you not to?

B        You make me feel unhappy. So unhappy. Every time.

A        I respect you enough to tell you the truth

B        Every time we meet, you *go* at me.

A       Too challenging for you?

B       I'm tired of it yes.

A       Break up with her, you'll feel better.

B       I love her.

A       Really?

B       I'm staying with her for ever.

A       Then you're not – no I don't want to say that but –

B       What?

A       No no… what do you think's the plan? With the assault? Shelling tonight, then in the morning ground troops –

        B *grabs* A.

B       You've gone this far you've told me everyone I know thinks I'm making a stupid mistake including my own mother, and none of you have enough respect to say that if it's what I want, if I want to be with her, then you'll support it, like real friends would, no, instead you're all talking behind my fucking back. You've told me that, so now go the whole fucking way and say it: 'If I stay with her then I'm not…'? Not what?

A       The person I thought you were.

        B *lets go of* A.

        *They look at each other.*

        *Long pause.*

B       …

        B *looks at* A.

        *Long pause.*

        That's it.

        That's the end.

        *Then goes.*

        A *stands on stage. Alone.*

## 4.

**Pint**

B     I've got a friend. Mahmoud. He's from there – I met him when I went there to do a seminar five years ago, there was a group of us, and he was the translator and we got on well, so – anyway, we've emailed each other on and off since then, he was over about two years ago and we met up had a coffee, and you know that was good, we're not real friends but it's good, you know I think we both like the idea of having a friend in a different country. Then a year ago when the civil war started there, the uprising, I sent an email asking him what he thought. He said he would wait and see, it was too early to tell. Then the stories started coming out about the atrocities, the mass graves, and there was the bombing in the capital where I knew he lived, but I... I haven't told anyone else this... but we're doing truth so...

The more I heard these things, the violent things that were happening basically on his doorstep the less likely it was that I was going to email him, make contact, I'd always find something else to do, I'd somehow never get round to it, and six months later, when the whole fucking thing was a mess now and every town is overrun by troops of one side or another and millions of refugees and from what I can tell it's impossible to avoid it there. He must be involved, one way or another, but it's too late to email after all this time, it would be... and even if I did I don't have the language, I don't have a vernacular to talk in a way that would respect what he's going through, and to be honest, this is the real truth, I suspect knowing his beliefs and how passionate he was about freedom that he was one of the first to pick up a gun and that he's probably dead. But I still haven't emailed. I don't – feel a connection to a world like that – it's so different – I think subconsciously – I'm scared that if I email him – I become connected. If he replies I'm directly involved. If he doesn't then I'm emailing the dead.

So when I think of the conflict I think of that. Him.

Mahmoud.

Not the rolling news. That you see all the time.

But him. Wherever he is. Or his body.

I haven't told Hannah.

I never would. It's not her world.

She's a safe place where none of that exists.

And this might be terrible. But I like the place Hannah provides.

So if it's got to the point where I have to choose.

Between my best friend, my dead pen pal and the truth.

Or Hannah, and security, and the simplicity that she offers.

Well.

I'm sorry if I disappoint.

A *enters*.

| | |
|---|---|
| A | Hey! |
| B | Hi |
| A | You're here! |
| B | Yeah. |
| A | How you doing? It's me! |
| B | Yes. |
| A | It's you! |
| B | That's right. |
| A | It's you and me! |
| B | Can we stop this now? |
| A | You're looking well. |
| B | Not particularly. |
| A | Thinner. |

B      Been working out.

A      Yeah or not eating at least and these clothes they don't
       only look shit-hot they also look comfortable, that's
       the thing I can never do. I can never get my clothes
       looking as comfortable as other people's don't know
       what I'm doing wrong. I love this jacket.

B      Thanks.

A      ?

B      Oh. I mean well you... you also... er...

A      Too late.

       *Beat.*

       I just went to the bar got you a pint, thought you'd
       want one when you –

B      I'm driving.

A      Yeah right so you can have one right.

B      I'll just grab some water if that's okay.

A      You don't want it?

B      No you go for it.

A      Okay.

       A *drinks*.

       A parent though!

B      Yep.

A      Proper parental.

B      It doesn't actually feel weird though it feels exactly
       what we should be doing.

A      That's great. What's it going to be then?

B      We'll have to see.

A      You haven't checked?

B      Checked?

A      Don't they tell you now?

B       Oh! You mean –

A       Boy or girl.

B       Thought you meant what was she going to be when she grew up

A       No.

B       No I realise now.

A       So it's a girl.

B       Yeah.

A       Amazing.

B       And you know I don't mind at all what she wants to do when she grows up, that's the –

A       Yeah I wasn't asking that.

B       You… Okay.

        *Beat.*

A       And everything went alright with all the…

B       What?

A       Procedure. To make it all –

B       Yeah. Yeah. Hannah's doing well.

A       That's great.

        'Hannah'

        Fuck.

        I haven't seen you since that night.

B       I know.

A       When we went in. The night it started, you remember?

B       Of course I remember that was also the night you told me to split up with her.

A       Bloody mess isn't it.

B       I assume you mean the war.

A     If they thought it was going to be over quickly.

B     I think the assumption was that this would go on a very long time.

A     I don't know how they'll ever get out of it.

B     Yeah it's fun this conversation isn't it, because we could be talking about the war in another country where people are dying or about my relationship with the mother of my child.

      *Beat.*

A     You think it'll go on for a long time then?

B     The war?

A     Yes the war. I was always talking about the war. We did the bit about your baby now we're talking about something important.

      *Beat.*

B     I don't know enough about it really.

A     ?

B     The war.

A     No come on you do.

B     No.

A     Your subject.

B     Not so much, not now.

A     You must have an opinion unless you're a vegetable.

B     I think it's just – we're doing our best – so…

A     Doing our best.

B     I don't want to get into it.

      *Pause.*

A     I've been here a while, you know that.

B     I'm sorry I was late.

A       No problem but you should also know that I have had
        a head start, if I seem a bit – woo – it's because I met a
        friend another friend – I have another friend! – for
        lunch we had a good time we played on the quiz
        machine, we did well actually won twenty quid from
        it, spent it after that, on the booze, and yeah since it's
        now what, four –

B       Five

A       Five o'clock is it? Well I'm a few on you I expect.

B       I expect so.

A       Probably about a seven.

B       Okay.

A       You remember the

B       Yeah I remember.

A       The system we had

B       Okay.

        How are you generally?

A       'Generally.' Ha ha! I'm *generally* good. Love it –
        you've become so proper – okay well honest answer
        to your small talk – Generally no. Not so great. I left
        my job.

B       Why?

A       There was so much *paperwork*, you know, it's not why I
        signed up to be a teacher. There was this day, I was
        hauling another load of marking in through the door and
        I thought fuck it, you know I don't even get an evening.

B       You get holidays.

A       Yeah but in term time, I can never have an evening off
        till Friday not even to just sit with a beer I'm up all night
        – anyway so the next day I took my letter of resignation
        in and by the end of the month I was out of there.

B       Right.

A    We'll see what next, but for now I'm happy.

B    You said you weren't doing great.

A    Yeah well it's a big change so – I don't know –
     I'm okay.

B    How are you doing for money?

A    Aaaaaargh. It'll be *okay*, *jeeesuss*!

B    Did you talk to anyone about it?

A    'Talk it over' you mean?

B    Whether it was a good idea.

A    I knew what I wanted to do so it was fine I didn't need
     to do that.

B    Okay.

A    No one else's business.

B    Right.

     *Pause.*

A    You've become a bit of a prick haven't you?

     *Beat.*

     Why haven't we met up?

B    Because you call me a prick and that's not my idea
     of fun.

A    I called and texted.

B    And in both messages you said I was a twat.

A    Yeah but that's – that's just –

     I've always called you a twat.

     That's what you're called.

     We used to meet all the time.

B    Things change.

A    Fuck off things do not. She got her way.

B        It's my choice, all of this –

A        Don't be pathetic your choice. I can see you in there, I
         can see the person I know locked away pretending to
         be this well-dressed Mr Fucking Conventional and I
         want you to know that I will be there for you when you
         want I am waiting for you to come back. I realise that
         this is just a stage you're going through but I will be
         waiting for the real you when you come back.

         When the chips are down. I'll be there. For you. I will.

B        You're not alright.

A        What?

B        You're drinking too much. More than ever.

         *Beat.*

A        Is that a message from your wife?

B        No and we're actually not married.

A        Thought I might have missed the wedding don't know
         if I'd get an invite.

B        How much have you drunk today?

A        It's a Sunday. I'm allowed.

B        Because it's God's day?

A        If God hadn't wanted us to drink, he wouldn't have
         given us mouths. I like booze it's a wonderful car
         that takes me on adventures it genuinely does I do
         things I never would imagine, and I'm functioning
         extremely well.

B        You left your job.

A        It's you that's got the problem, that woman Hannah
         wife is she your wife?

B        I just told you a minute ago.

A        Did you? I forgot.

B        No she isn't.

A    Why not why isn't she your wife?

B    We don't believe in marriage.

A    Oh for fuck's sake okay. Well – jesus –whatever she is
     she's a much more destructive force in your life than
     Mr Booze is for me, me and Mr Booze we have a
     lovely time, mostly, we do – fuck. Oh – Ha!

B    Be careful.

A    I hit myself in the face – did you see that? I actually
     just hit myself in the face with my own hand. I am a
     dick. I'm like halfway through telling you I'm fine and
     I hit myself in the eye with my fist. What a penis.

B    Would you like to see someone?

A    Who?

B    I'll pay for you to get some help.

A    Someone who'll help me not to hit myself in the face
     with my own hand.

B    Someone to help you with the –

A    You used to laugh, if I'd hit myself in the face before
     you would have pissed your fucking pants laughing at
     me, now it's all, oh oh get some help.

B    It's not funny.

A    Yeah but it is though. I just hit myself in my own face.
     Like this. It's funny.

B    No.

A    You've fucked your life up.

B    *I* have?

A    You were better before.

B    You can't keep your limbs out of your face and *I'm* the
     one who –

A    Before Hannah, you were nicer, more fun, even a bit
     fatter, which was also, actually, better. But now, with

her, and this *baby*, you've taken the wrong path. And it's too late to go back. So thanks, but I'm fine for help, you just worry about what the fuck you're going to do.

B    Well this is what I wanted to say actually.

A    Right then say it then

B    When I have a kid, and you know we might have more than one

A    Awww

B    But even if it's just my daughter, once she's born, I can't be there for her and Hannah – I can't be there for my family, and you.

A    You're not there for me.

B    I can't emotionally support you like I used to. I don't have the bandwidth.

A    'Bandwidth.' Anyway – you don't. Any more. We never see each other. I tried calling you.

B    When?

A    The night before I quit my job I tried calling like three times I wanted to talk and you didn't pick up, all I got late in the evening like half eleven was a polite little fucking text saying 'Hi – sorry – hope all's good. Sorry I missed you. Will call soon.' That was it. And you didn't. Call. Soon or otherwise. But I needed to talk. You could see it was me on the phone and you left it ringing. I don't fit with your world.

*Beat.*

Is that why you agreed to meet?

B    What?

A    To tell me that you won't be there for me in the future.

B    No. I just thought we could have a drink.

But I realised on the way, I should let you know.

A      Well you have. I will no longer. Lean on you. When the chips are down, for me, don't worry, I will fuck off somewhere else.

B

A

B      Sorry but

A

B

A

*Long pause.*

B      You know what they found.

By that village.

You know when they got there, what they found?

A      Yeah.

It's not getting better is it?

*Pause.*

B      They washed down the river. Did you hear that?

All the bits had washed down the river.

**5.**

**Ladder**

A *enters with an A-frame ladder and opens it.*

*Climbs the ladder. Looks around.*

*Nearly cries. Unsteady.*

*Stops herself.*

*Comes down the ladder and stands.*

*Gets out the harmonica. Plays it badly.*

*Stops. Hears* B *approaching and puts it away.*

B *enters.*

*They look at each other.*

A     You look like shit.

B     So do you.

A     No I look like crap you look like shit. I look like I haven't changed out of these clothes for three days which is actually the situation, and therefore we use the expression crap –

B     Okay.

A     whereas you look like someone has beaten you up and dumped you somewhere you look like you've been through some kind of massive trauma and that's a very different situation where we would say you 'look like shit'.

B     Can I come in?

A     You are in.

B     Right. The door was –

      Sorry.

      What's that doing there?

A

B     How are you?

A       Really good.

        *Pause.*

        Oh. Sorry. 'How are you?'

B       I'm in trouble.

A       Clearly.

B       The chips are – the shit has

A       The chips have hit the fan?

B       And you said, if I needed to –

A       What's happened?

B       Can I have a drink?

A       Sure.

B       Are you –

A       No. I've – oh, you probably don't know. I don't
        any more.

        I don't drink.

B       Oh.

A       It turned out it was an all-or-nothing situation I would
        either drink everything in the fucking place, or I
        wouldn't drink, and in the end, after an incident
        involving myself and a night and a pavement, I
        decided my dignity couldn't hack it, let alone my liver,
        so we all, my dignity my liver and me, decided to pack
        it in, so I'm afraid I don't have very much drink in the
        house the only thing I have is that bottle of port, the
        second half of that bottle of port you bought me, you
        remember you could have some of that. I kept it. Out
        of some kind of –

        oh fuck it well because I missed you and it reminded
        me, laugh now.

B       She told me to leave.

A       Yeah course she did, figured that out.

B       I don't want a drink, I'm just really unhappy.

A       Okay.

B       She said I couldn't have contact with my daughter any
        more. And she – she's been seeing someone else. She
        said I wasn't who she thought I was, that she'd had
        enough of me letting her down.

A       Sorry.

B       No you're not.

A       No alright. You should be celebrating. She was terrible.
        This is a good day for you.

B       You redecorating?

A       No.

        *Pause.*

B       Sorry.

        I know it's probably strange but.

        I didn't know where else to come.

        *Pause.*

        She didn't understand why I kept on watching the news.

A       You were watching the news? Well done.

B       You know coverage of what's going on. She said it
        wasn't appropriate in a house with a newborn baby to be
        inflicting that level of noise and violence, and it was that
        that made me finally lose it I said but you watch all
        these horror movies with our daughter right there on
        your lap, you watch *Saw IV* while you're fucking
        breastfeeding – people screaming getting their legs cut
        off while you're there with our newborn daughter and
        she said it's different and I said how and she said
        because it's not real life. And it's starting to get
        dangerous, this conflict, it's spreading into other
        countries she said and she didn't like it, can you please
        switch it off she said and I didn't, and then she started to
        cry and I shouted and she shouted back and it got hotter
        than it ever has and she told me that this was it, and she
        was going to be honest and she'd been seeing someone
        else, since even before the baby, and – oh fuck –

A     Right.

B     She said I had to leave. So I did.

A     And then you spend the night in a skip?

B     The car.

A     That makes more sense. Are you cold?

B     No.

A     You're shaking.

B     Oh.

A     Like a washing machine: gu gu gu gu gu gu

B     Shock or something.

A     Serves you right.

B     What?

A

B     Sorry. Sorry. You're probably busy. I'm intruding.

A     Yeah but it doesn't matter.

B     You alright though?

      Have you got a job yet?

A     I've made all sorts of applications, it's looking good.

B     Okay. That's great. I'm proud of you.

A     Well I'm proud of you too.

B     What?

A     Watching the news so much. It's the first glimmer of
      conscience in you for a long time. That wasn't true
      what I just said I haven't put in any applications I don't
      want a job, I just stay in mostly.

B     Oh.

A     Don't see very many people at all these days. Don't
      you like this, you love this don't you? Us two, like old
      times, come on, you've missed it.

B       Was it because of what I said? That you got some help,
        with the drink?

A       No.

B       Right.

A       It had nothing to do with you I did it all myself.

B       Okay. Sure. That's... well of course that's completely
        true in the end.

A

B

A

B       You were right.

        You were right about everything.

A

B       I mean her.

A

B       She's been – oh –

A

B       Shit. Sorry.

        A *goes and gets a bottle of tequila.*

        What's that?

        A *opens the bottle.*

        You said you didn't drink any more.

        Are you getting that for me?

        Cos I really don't want –

A       No it's not for you.

        A *drinks from the bottle.*

        So I'm one of those people who when they get really
        very drunk, they come out the other side and obtain a
        kind of clarity, at least for a while, and that's where I am
        now. I'm so pissed if you lit a match I would inflame.

I'm currently a nine I reckon. I lied. Earlier. A lot. I'm a fucking mess.

*Beat.*

B     Can I have some?

A     No.

*Pause.*

You know whose fault all this drinking is?

B     Mine.

A     Mostly.

*A climbs the ladder.*

B     You should be careful.

A     What?

B     If you're that drunk. You might fall off.

A     Oh yeah. Thanks. I'll be careful.

*A pulls a piece of string, and a noose falls down at exactly the right height.*

B     What the fuck.

A     Yeah.

B     What the fuck are you doing?

*A puts the noose over her head.*

A     I've been thinking about it for a long time, even went to the length of getting the rope and stuff, apparently if you get the weight right, which I have, it's the quickest way, and I don't have anything, I don't have a job, I don't go out, not in a relationship, with anyone, any more. I'm not... not happy at all, life is... For the last four months I've been calling you again and again and despite what I said last time you've been ignoring me. But then earlier today when *you* call, *I* answer, and you say can I come over, and I can tell in your voice that things are not good I know what's happened, so I say okay without thinking, and you say thanks and that's it, but I didn't get to say any

of what I'm *feeling* right now, when I really should,
and you're on your way, and I get this idea – as I drink
a bit more – this idea that I'll unlock the door, and
then do it, and you'll walk in and find me hanging,
swinging, and you'll know it happened after you
called me and you'll blame yourself. For ever.

B    Just wait.

A    Which you should, but you must have got a cab here or
something because you were too quick and I wasn't
ready, you even fucked this up for me.

B    Yeah I got a cab.

A    Tory fucking traitor. You used to walk.

*The ladder wobbles.*

B    Careful.

A    Careful? You know what I'm about *to do*? Shit.

B    But I don't understand why, you're not – you're not
that bad, things aren't –

A    I'm doing it because in the end when you're struggling
to find someone to share your life with, and money is
*tough* and you do have a problem with alcohol and
other people start to avoid you, you rely on one thing –
your close friends, these other people, to make it
bearable, and when you find that one of them is not the
person you thought they were, when they support a
military assault that will kill lots of people, and then
when because of that they find a woman who is
unsuitable for them, and then they stop talking to you,
then what else have I got?

What else is there?

Right.

B    No.

A    Right.

A *goes to kick the ladder away* – B *holds on to it.*

Get off. You can't stop me.

B        No.

         *A starts kicking at the ladder. B holds firm.*

A        Get off the fucking –

B        No!

A        It's my decision!

B        You can't.

A        Just because you need me again that's the only reason.

B        I'm sorry.

A        Too late. Fuck off! Aaaar!

         *In the scuffle, B moves, the ladder tips, A wobbles on
         the top, and falls.*

B        No!

         *B catches A's legs and supports them from underneath,
         on his shoulders.*

A        Get off! Let me fall!

B        No!

A        Let me go!

B        No!

         *A now has the noose relatively tight round her neck.
         B is underneath, just able to support the weight.*

A        Get off!

B        No. Stop. Stop kicking me.

         *More of a scuffle.*

A        Fucking...

         *Eventually A stops kicking, and it settles.*

         *A moment.*

B        Can you breathe?

A        ...

B     *Can you breathe!*

A     *Yes!* Unfortunately, yes.

B     Right.

      *Beat.*

      Good.

      *Pause.*

      Right.

      *Pause.*

A     You know you've really messed this up. It's the force
      of the fall that severs the spinal column. It doesn't
      sound nice, but apparently it's that that makes it
      relatively painless. When you let go, all that'll happen
      now is that I'll slowly choke to death and it'll be
      fucking horrific so thanks a bunch.

B     I'm not going to let go.

A     You can't stay holding me up like that for ever.

B     I'll call the police.

A     Your phone's in your coat. Over there. And if you
      move, that's it.

      *Beat.*

B     I'll shout for help.

A     Be my guest.

B     …

A     Go on then.

B     I will. Wait.

A     ?

B     Help!

      *Beat.*

      Help!

      *Pause.*

Help!

*Pause.*

I feel really stupid.

A     They won't hear you.

Even if they do. People round here.

They won't get involved.

Especially if someone's shouting for help.

Run a mile.

*Pause.*

B     Help!

*Pause.*

Help.

*Pause.*

It's not working.

*Beat.*

A     Just let go.

B     No. I saw this documentary, it was on the Discovery Channel I think –

A     Of course it was –

B     About people jumping off a bridge, to commit suicide, and apparently the ones that survived, all of them, when talking about it afterwards, they all regretted it at the last minute, they all spoke of how just as they fell, they realised they'd made a terrible mistake. Luckily of course those ones survived, but the tragedy is all the ones who felt that, who had that thought, when it was too late, when there was nothing they could do –

A     What's your point?

B     Did you feel that, when you fell?

A     In the moment the ladder went?

B     Yes.

A     No. I was hoping it would be all over.

B     And now?

A     Oh…

*She cries.*

God. Please.

*Please.* Just let me go.

*Please!*

B     You don't want to die.

A     Yeah I do. I do. I really do.

B     I'll be there. For you. From now on. Whatever. I promise.

A     Guilt.

B     I messed it up I know I should've done something.

But I thought it's your decisions, you're an adult and…

Please. At least come down. And we'll talk about it.

And then if you still want to. Well I can't stop you for ever can I?

Yeah?

Come down. Please.

You dick.

You complete…

Fucking… .

Dick

A     What are you doing?

B     Don't know. Banter.

A

B

A

B

A        Yeah okay I'll come down.

B        Okay. So get the noose off your neck before I –

A        Yeah *alright*, give me a minute.

         *A tries to reach up and remove the noose but it's too tight.*

B        Careful. You're twisting.

A        I'm trying to remove the thing.

B        Just take it off.

A        It's too tight.

B        Jesus Christ…

A        Can you lift me up any more?

B        No.

A        *Try.*

B        I am

A        Try properly.

B        Shut up – wait –

         *He does, but can't.*

A        Come on!

B        *I'm doing my best!*

         *A keeps trying. Then stops.*

A        No. I can't do it.

         *They settle back to the original position.*

         *Beat.*

B        Great.

         *Beat.*

         Really good.

A        This is your fault.

B        Now what?

         *Pause.*

A          Is there any furniture you can –

B          No I can't reach anything.

           *Pause.*

A          Well that's it then.

B          No.

A          You'll eventually get tired and sink slowly down and that'll be the end.

B          No.

           Wait.

           B *sees the remote control on the floor.*

           B *tries to reach it with his foot.*

A          What are you doing?

B          Wait.

           B *scrapes the remote over to him with his foot, then starts to take off one shoe with the other foot.*

A          What the fuck are you doing?

B          The remote control.

A          What about it?

B          It's on the floor.

A          The… what? How's that going to help? Great. We can watch TV.

           At least as I die I won't get bored.

           Go on. Put it on. Might be something good.

B          Just shut up.

           B *uses his foot without the shoe to switch on the television.*

           *There are sudden sounds and images of war. Quite quiet.*

           *It takes them both by surprise for a moment.*

           *They watch.*

A        Fuck. Look at it.

         Oh.

         You're not shaking any more.

B        Puts it in perspective doesn't it?

A        What puts what in perspective?

B        Everything.

A        How can *anything* possibly put *everything* in
         perspective?

B        That's why I was watching it in the first place, the
         news, I found at home, when Hannah was being – oh
         jesus – it's been shit for a long time okay? You were
         right – but I found that weirdly if I put on the news it
         would calm me down.

         It would calm me down because I'd know that what
         was happening to me everything in my life every
         single thing was lucky. Compared to that.

         To that. Horror. All the problems I had were…

         Now it's not just that country but others and it might.

         You know they say it might…

         And having a baby.

         You think. What's going to happen?

         What can we do? To protect ourselves.

A        Stop wobbling.

B        Sorry. Sorry.

         Right. Right.

         *They watch it for a moment.*

         When we get you down, can I stay?

A        No.

B        Really though.

A        No you really can't, fucking freeloader find your own
         place. Jesus.

B     I'll sleep on the sofa.

A     You won't. I need that sofa for occasional sitting.

      You can go back to your *car*.

      *Pause.*

      Yes alright you can stay.

      *Pause.*

      This is tight.

      *Pause.*

      You're getting tired.

B     No.

      *Pause.*

A     What's the idea then?

B     You've got a massive subwoofer.

A     I beg your pardon.

B     Subwoofer.

A     You're just making sounds now.

B     The speaker system you have it's really good and it has
      a massive bass speaker, you probably never have it
      loud enough to notice, but if I turn the television up
      enough it will shake through the building with the
      noise and someone will eventually get angry and call
      the police, or the warden downstairs or they might
      come up and bang on the door themselves, but either
      way, when they do, we can shout at them for help, tell
      them to break it down and help us.

A     That's a terrible idea.

B     Anything better?

A     Just do it.

      B *starts to turn the volume up on the TV. The sound of
      war and bombing gets louder and louder.*

      *It gets to full volume.*

*They watch.*

*Then shout over it.*

B    I'm really sorry. About everything.

A    Just don't let me down.

B    I won't. I promise. Ever. Never again.

A    No. I mean really… you're…

B    Oh. Right.

Yeah.

A    You're slipping.

*B lifts up A a bit.*

B    Better?

A    Yeah.

I'll always drink. Won't I?

*B reaches out his hand. A takes it.*

*B is crying.*

*Pause.*

Love you.

B    You too.

*The bombing and fighting sound.*

*Banging.*

*Louder and louder.*

*Blackout.*

*End.*

**A Nick Hern Book**

*An Intervention* first published in Great Britain in 2014 as a paperback original by Nick Hern Books Limited, The Glasshouse, 49a Goldhawk Road, London W12 8QP, in association with Paines Plough and Watford Palace Theatre

*An Intervention* copyright © 2014 Mike Bartlett

Mike Bartlett has asserted his right to be identified as the author of this work

Cover image by Nick Scott (www.narcsville.co.uk)

Designed and typeset by Nick Hern Books, London
Printed in Great Britain by CPI Group (UK) Ltd

A CIP catalogue record for this book is available from the British Library

ISBN 978 1 84842 383 1